THE NEEDLEPOINT AND CROSS-STITCH

DIRECTORY

JAN EATON AND LIZ MUNDLE

A QUINTET BOOK

ISBN: 1–85348–848–8

This book was designed and produced by
Quintet Publishing Limited

Creative Director: Peter Bridgewater
Art Director: Ian Hunt
Designer: James Lawrence
Editor: Caroline Beattie
Photographer: Andrew Sydenham
Illustrators: Julia Milne, Nicki Simmonds
Jacket Design: Nik Morley

Typeset in Great Britain by
Central Southern Typesetters, Eastbourne

Produced in Australia by Griffin Colour

Published by Selectabook Limited,
Devizes.

Contents

Fabrics

Fabrics for embroidery fall into three distinct categories: plain-weave fabrics, even-weave fabrics and canvas.

Plain-weave fabrics

Only plain-weave fabrics with a regular woven or printed pattern such as gingham, polka-dots or stripes will provide a useful grid for working crossed stitches neatly and evenly. The main exception is the herringbone family of stitches, which lend themselves to being worked freely on most plain-weave fabrics including sheer ones. Basic cross stitch and some other canvas stitches can be worked on an unpatterned plain-weave fabric, such as medium-weight cotton, wool or silk, providing piece of canvas is tacked over the fabric first, to provide a grid for regular stitching. When the embroidery is completed the canvas grid is removed.

The most important consideration in working embroidery on a plain-weave fabric is to match the weight of the thread and needle to the fabric. The thread should not be heavy enough to distort the fabric weave or pull it out of shape, leaving puckers in the background. A firmly woven fabric should be chosen that allows the thread to pass easily in and out and is strong enough to bear the weight of solid areas of stitching without distortion. Knitted fabrics or loosely woven fabrics which stretch are not suitable for hand embroidery.

Even-weave fabrics

Even-weave fabrics, the second group, are also plain-weave fabrics but there is an important difference. The warp and weft threads are identical in thickness and provide the same number of threads in a given area, enabling cross stitch to be worked accurately by the method of counting the threads. Single even-weave fabrics are made from single strands of intersecting threads; the thickness of the threads dictates the thread count. One of the most useful fabrics is Glenshee linen, with a count of 29 threads per inch (2.5 cm). Counted stitches can be worked over different numbers of threads depending on your preference for the size of the finished stitch. For example, basic cross stitch worked over three threads of Glenshee fabric will produce just under 10 stitches per inch.

There is a large range of similar even-weave fabrics available, some finer and some coarser than Glenshee, and they are usually made from linen, cotton or wool, or blends of these with polyester or other synthetics. They are mainly produced in white, cream or pastel colours. Special types of even-weave fabrics suitable for counted thread techniques are Hardanger, Aida and Binca. Hardanger fabric has pairs of threads woven together while Aida and Binca have four threads woven together to form distinct blocks in the weave over which the stitches are formed. These fabrics come in different thread counts and are usually made of pure cotton, or cotton and synthetic blends. The colour range includes pastels and bright colours such as yellow, red and green.

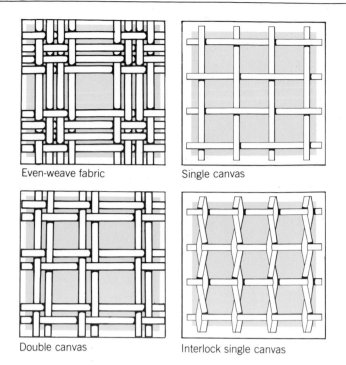

Even-weave fabric

Single canvas

Double canvas

Interlock single canvas

Canvas

The third fabric group consists of different types of canvas. Canvas is made of vertical and horizontal threads woven together to produce precisely spaced holes between the threads. The points at which the threads intersect are known as meshes and the fabric has a regular grid-like structure. Most canvas is made of stiffened cotton, but soft linen canvas and very fine silk gauze are also available. Rigid plastic canvas with a coarse mesh can be bought in rectangular sheets or cut into shapes. Cotton canvas is available in white, ecru or yellow. It is advisable to use white canvas when the embroidery threads are very pale as the stitching may not conceal the canvas completely; otherwise use ecru or yellow, as with darker-toned threads the canvas is less likely to show through the stitching. If you are using dark colours over a large area, the canvas can be painted to match to avoid any showthrough.

Choose the best canvas you can afford as the cheaper types often have knots or unevenly twisted threads in the weave which can distort the stitching. There are two main types of canvas: single canvas (Mono) and double canvas (also known as Penelope canvas). Single plain canvas is formed by the intersection of a single vertical and horizontal thread. Interlock single canvas has a locked construction which makes it more stable than the plain canvas; each vertical thread is made up of two thin threads twisted around each other and round a single, thicker horizontal thread so each mesh is 'locked' into place. All crossed canvaswork stitches can be worked on single canvas but some, such as the basic cross stitch and fishbone stitch, are more successful when worked on double canvas.

Double canvas is similar to single canvas except that the mesh is formed by pairs of vertical and horizontal threads. Canvas comes in a large number of sizes, or gauges. The gauge of a canvas is the number of threads which can be stitched in an inch (2.5 cm); for example

24 gauge canvas has 24 threads to every inch. Fine silk gauze has a gauge of up to 72 per inch for delicate work, and the cotton canvases range right up to coarse rug canvas with a 3 or 5 gauge. If you work from a chart and use a larger gauge canvas than suggested, the finished piece will be larger; alternatively, a finer canvas will reduce the size of the piece. With canvaswork, it is extremely important to match the weight of threads with the gauge of the canvas to avoid crammed, bulky stitching or, if the threads are too thin, canvas covered unevenly by the stitching.

Needles

Needles for hand embroidery are of three types: crewel, chenille and tapestry. They have longer eyes than do needles used for plain sewing, to make threading a thick thread easier. All needles are numerically graded from fine to coarse, the higher numbers being the finer needles. Exact choice of needle is largely down to personal preference, but the eye of the needle should accommodate the thread easily and should be the right size to draw the thread through the fabric or canvas without pulling it out of shape. You will soon discover by 'feel' which size and type of needle suits the work you are doing.

Crewel needles — sizes 1 to 10 — are sharp, medium length needles with a large eye and are used for fine and medium-weight embroidery on plain-weave fabrics.

Chenille needles — sizes 14 to 26 — are also pointed, but are longer, thicker and have larger eyes than crewel needles and are used with heavier threads and fabrics.

Tapestry needles — sizes 14 to 26 — are similar in size to chenille needles, but with a blunt end instead of a sharp point. They are used for canvaswork and embroidery on even-weave fabrics; the blunt end separates the threads of the fabric to pass through, whereas a sharp needle would split them.

Threads

Embroidery threads are made in a wide range of weights and colours. Some are twisted and must be used as one thread, while others are made up of several strands which can be separated and used singly or put together in different weight or colour combinations. For cross stitch embroidery on plain- or even-weave fabric, the following threads are suitable:

Stranded cotton — a loosely twisted, slightly shiny six-strand thread which can be separated for fine work. A good all-purpose thread with an extensive colour range.

Pearl cotton — a twisted 2-ply thread with a lustrous sheen, which cannot be divided. It comes in sizes 3, 5 and 8, 3 being the heaviest, and in a good range of colours.

Soft embroidery cotton — a tightly twisted 5-ply thread, fairly thick and with a matt finish. It is used as a single thread on heavier fabrics.

Coton a broder — a tightly twisted thread which is similar to pearl cotton, although softer, finer and with a less lustrous finish.

Stranded pure silk — a seven-stranded, shiny thread which can be divided. It comes in an extensive colour range including many brilliant shades not available in stranded cotton. It is also available as twisted thread, in a much narrower colour range. Pure silk is difficult to work with and must be drycleaned.

For canvaswork, wool yarns are usually preferred as they are more hard wearing, with stranded cotton, silk and pearl cotton introduced as highlights. For articles that do not require a hard-wearing finish, such as pictures, any of the previous threads can be used on their own. Crewel and Persian wools are suitable for even-weave fabrics, providing the fabric is loose enough to allow the thread to pass through easily, without shredding or fraying.

The wools most widely available are:

Crewel wool — a fine 2-ply wool for delicate canvaswork, in a wide range of subtle colours. Two, three or four strands can be used together on coarse canvas.

Persian wool — a loosely twisted three-strand wool which can be divided. Each strand is slightly thicker than crewel wool and the colours are brighter.

Tapestry wool — a tightly twisted 4-ply wool used singly on coarse canvas.

Frames

All cross stitch embroidery, whether on fabric or canvas, should be kept taut during the stitching. The easiest way to do this is to pin or staple the fabric to a simple wooden stretcher a few inches longer than the finished size of the piece of work. G-clamps can be used to hold this type of frame securely on the edge of a table, leaving both hands free for working. Work on plain-weave fabric can be stretched on a two-ringed circular hoop which can be moved easily from one area of fabric to another. More sophisticated frames, some with integral stands are also available. Good lighting, preferably from an anglepoise lamp, is important and you need a comfortable chair of the right height for you to work easily at a frame without overstretching.

Other equipment

Every embroiderer will accumulate a personal collection of particularly useful items of equipment and these may vary according to the type of work and the materials preferred. There are a number of general sewing aids which will invariably be useful — dressmaking scissors, a small, sharp pair of embroidery scissors with short blades, a thimble, a tape measure, ordinary sewing needles and threads for tacking and a box of dressmaking pins. For design work and preparing the fabric you will need drawing pins or a lightweight but strong staple gun; pencils, felt-tip pens, markers and acrylic paints; a good supply of tracing and graph paper; a ruler and a set square; and last but not least, a small mirror is a useful item, enabling you to work out reverse motifs and the corners of borders.

Separating stranded threads (*right*) Tease out one end of the thread and take two of the strands in your mouth, holding the other strands in one hand. With your free hand take hold of the other end of the thread. Gently pull the divided strands apart, while firmly sliding your other hand down the length of thread. It is important to keep this three-way contact to ensure that the threads do not entangle as they unravel.

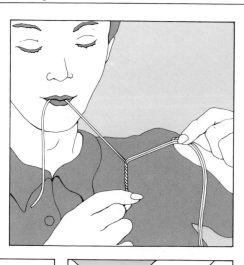

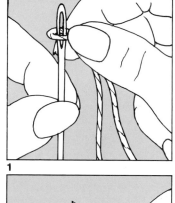

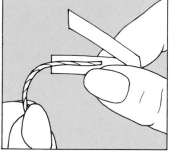

Threading the needle
Loop method (top)
1 Loop the end of the thread round the needle and pull tight.
2 Slip the loop off the needle and push it through the eye of the needle.

Paper strip method (above)
1 Cut a strip of paper, with a width just less than the length of the needle eye, and the length about 2 in (5 cm). Fold the strip in half and place the end of the thread inside the paper.
2 Feed the folded paper with the thread inside through the eye of the needle.

Preparing the fabric

Any type of fabric or canvas should be finished at the edges before the embroidery is begun, to prevent it fraying and to strengthen the edges for mounting the fabric in a frame. When working out the size of the fabric needed for a design, allow 3 in (7.5 cm) extra all round for unframed pieces and 5 in (12.5 cm) for framed ones. Cut the fabric to the correct size, using sharp scissors, following the grainlines or canvas threads carefully. To finish off the raw edges, turn them over and hemstitch them by hand or machine. On closely woven fabric the raw edges can be finished with a row of machine zigzag stitches. To neaten and secure canvas, cotton tape should be folded over the edges and stitched down firmly.

Preparing threads

Working threads should be used in lengths of approximately 15 in (38 cm). Longer threads will tend to fray or lose their sheen because they are pulled through the fabric too often. A skein of thread can be cut into convenient lengths before you begin to stitch. Cut a piece of card 15 in (38 cm) long, wrap the thread round and round the length of the card, not too tightly, and cut through the thread at each end. Cut lengths can be loosely plaited to prevent them tangling and each length removed as needed by gently pulling one end from the plait.

Threading the needle

There are three ways to simplify threading a needle, especially for coarser threads. The first method is to use a needlethreader — a flat piece of metal with a diamond-shaped loop of fine wire at one end. Pass the wire loop through the eye of the needle, place the thread through the loop and then draw the loop back through the needle, pulling the thread with it. If a needlethreader is not available, use either the loop or paper strip method illustrated.

Starting and finishing the thread

When you start stitching, do not use a knot as this may show through the finished piece or make a bump on the right side, especially if the work is to be framed. Anchor the thread by making one or two tiny back stitches in a space that will be covered as the stitching progresses. Alternatively, leave a tail of approximately 2 in (5 cm) of thread which can be darned in later. If you are continuing to work an area which is partly stitched, anchor a new thread by sliding the needle under the wrong side of a group of stitches, securing about an inch (2.5 cm) of the thread underneath them. To finish a thread, slide the needle in the same way under a group of stitches and cut off the loose end of thread.

Round frames *(right)*
1 To prevent damage to fine fabric, wrap a length of cotton tape around the inner ring. Make sure it is tightly wound, then secure the ends with masking tape.
2 Place the fabric over the inner ring with the design facing upwards. Then place the outer ring over the top and adjust the screw so that it will fit lightly around the inner ring.
3 With your hands, gradually work your way around the ring, pressing it down over the fabric and inner ring, making sure the fabric is kept taut by pulling it outwards with your fingers and thumbs.
4 You may find that the outer ring rides up as you are pulling on the fabric. In this case push the ring down over the inner circle so that it is securely fitted. When the fabric is evenly taut, tighten the screw to hold the outer ring firmly in place.

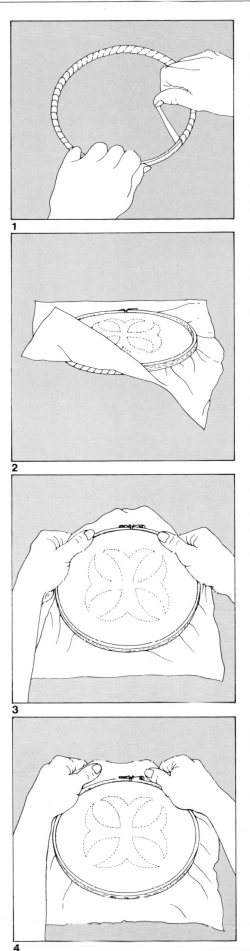

Using embroidery frames

There are several types of embroidery frame available, and the choice depends both on the size of the piece and your own preference. A hand-held round frame is adequate for a small piece of embroidery, but a large piece will require a rectangular frame with either a stand or clamps to keep it steady. A frame with a stand also gives the advantage that both your hands are left free for working.

Round frames

Round frames, or hoops, are used for small pieces of embroidery worked on plain-weave fabrics. They come in various sizes, in two sections which are placed one inside the other with the fabric sandwiched in between and tightened by a screw at the side. The smaller hoop, without the screw, should be bound with thin cotton tape as a precaution against the fabric working loose and sagging as the embroidery is stitched. The tape will also protect delicate fabrics. To mount the fabric, spread it over the smaller hoop and press the larger hoop down over it. Tighten the screw on the outer hoop slightly until it fits snugly round the small hoop, then ease the fabric with your fingers until it is evenly stretched and taut. Tighten the screw fully.

If the design is too large to fit completely inside the frame, the fabric can be moved along after one portion is completed. To protect the stitches already worked, spread a piece of tissue paper or muslin over the embroidery before it is remounted in the frame and cut away the paper or muslin carefully to expose the next area to be stitched. Release the fabric from the frame whenever you stop work for any long period; loosen the screw and remove the larger hoop.

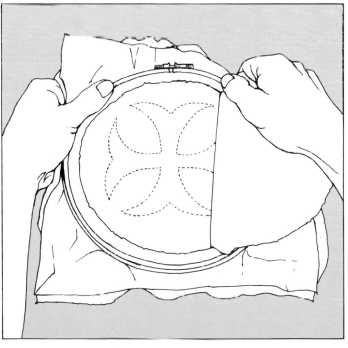

Protection of fabric or stitches *(above)*
The rings may damage the fabric or stitching already worked. To avoid this, lay a piece of tissue paper over the fabric. Put the outer ring in place and secure it. Tear away the paper in the centre.

Rectangular frames for all fabrics and canvas

The simplest rectangular frame is a wooden stretcher. You can make one from four wood battens joined at the corners, or you will find them available in many sizes from art shops. The size of frame you need is determined by the size of the fabric you are working on, as a stretcher is not adjustable. Leave a good margin on the fabric to make sure the entire area of the design is well clear of the inner edges of the stretcher. Mark the centre of each side of the stretcher and the centre of each edge of the fabric. Starting at the centre of one side of the stretcher, line up the marks and pin or staple the fabric to this side, working from the centre outwards. Then attach the opposite side of the fabric to the stretcher, again working outwards from the centre, making sure the grain of the fabric is not distorted. Fasten the two remaining sides in the same way.

Slate frames and rotating frames are more sophisticated than the simple stretcher and are bought from embroidery suppliers. They have the advantage of being adjustable and also of stretching the fabric very evenly. Each type of frame consists of top and bottom rollers with strips of webbing attached, and two side pieces secured with nuts, screws or pegs. After marking the centre on both the rollers and the top and bottom of the fabric, stitch the fabric securely to the webbing, working from the centre point outwards each time. Use back stitch or herringbone stitch and a strong thread such as buttonhole thread. Slot the sides into the rollers, pull the fabric taut and secure the fixing device. If the fabric is too long, take up the slack by winding it around one of the rollers. Lace the sides of the fabric to the sides of the frame using a strong needle and fine string or linen carpet thread and leave a length of string at top and bottom. Tighten the lacing from the centre outwards, working each side alternately to give an equal pull on the fabric. Secure each end of the string by knotting it round the frame. It is important to get an even tension over the whole surface of the fabric, and several adjustments may be needed.

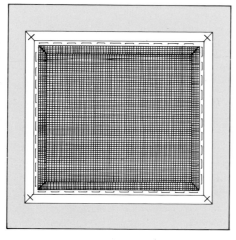

Canvas stretcher (above) This simple rectangular frame is made from four wood battens, joined up at the corners. The fabric is stretched and fastened lengthways, and then across the frame.

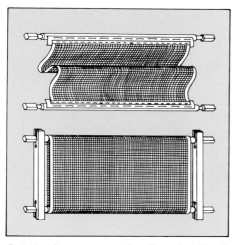

Rotating frame (above)
1 Sew the top and bottom of the canvas to the webbing.
2 Loosen the nuts on the side arms to open the slits and slot in all four ends of the side arms. Turn the rods to take up the slack canvas. Tighten the nuts on the side arms.

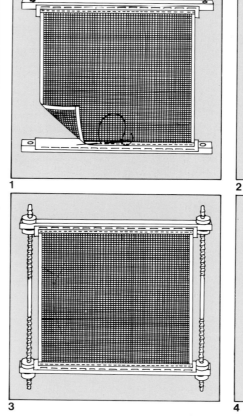

1

2

3

4

Slate frame (above)
1 Bind the canvas to prevent the edges fraying. Mark the centres of each rod and each edge of the canvas. Matching the centres, stitch the top of the canvas to the webbing on one rod, working from the centre outwards. Repeat for the bottom edge.
2 Fit two locking nuts to the centre of each side arm. Fold or roll the canvas to just over half the length of the side arms. Slot the top of the side arms into the holes in the top rod; then slot into the bottom rod in the same way. Push the locking nuts towards the rods.
3 Draw the rods along the side arms so the canvas is fully extended. Push the centred nuts close to the rods and apply locking nuts to the ends of each side arm. Tighten the nuts on both sides of top and bottom rods to hold the canvas taut.
4 To stretch the canvas at either side, oversew between the side arms and edges of the canvas using long, slanting stitches. Before finishing the thread, pull on each stitch from the beginning of the sewing to tighten it and make sure the canvas is evenly stretched. Secure the thread at each corner of the frame.

Reducing a design
(right)
1 Trace your design on to the centre of a piece of paper.
2 Draw a large grid over the design, with lines approximately 1 in (2.5 cm) apart.
3 With a straightedge, mark the chosen proportions for the outer edges of your design.
4 Draw in a diagonal line across the grid from corner to corner.
5 Tape a piece of paper, smaller than the full design, on top of the grid, securing it at the bottom lefthand corner. Extend the diagonal line showing at the top right of the grid down over the taped piece of paper.
6 Extend the bottom line of your original design perimeter to meet the diagonal in the bottom left corner. Draw a vertical line from this corner at right angles to meet up with the line on the lefthand side of the grid.
7 Measure the desired width of the new design from the lefthand corner along the bottom line. From this point, draw a line up at right angles to meet the diagonal. Then, draw a line at right angles to this vertical line, to meet the lefthand side of the design, completing the box.
8 On the original grid, number the squares across the top and down the sides.
9 Divide the small box into the same number of squares, making a small grid proportionate to the large one.
10 and **11** To reproduce the design, copy the lines in the boxes on the original grid onto the corresponding squares of the smaller grid. It is easier to reproduce the design accurately by marking the points on each square where the design crosses the grid lines and then joining up these points.

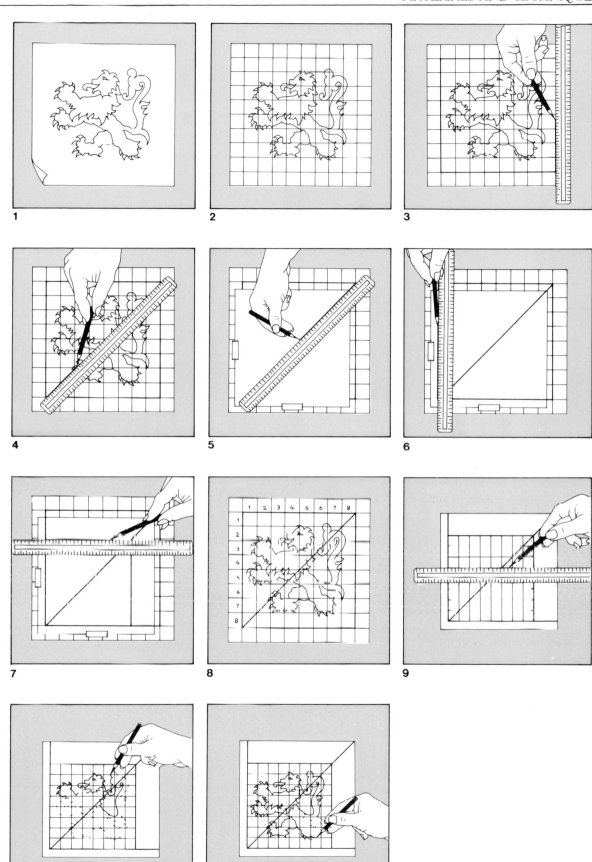

1

2

3

4

5

6

7

8

9

10

11

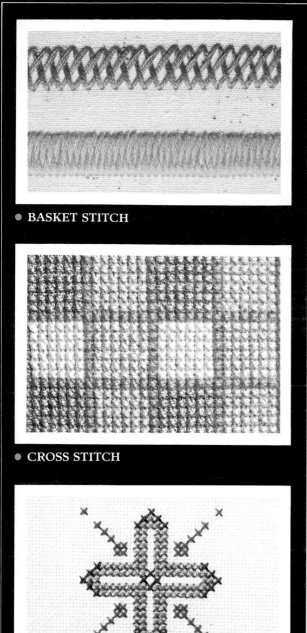

● **BASKET STITCH**

● **CROSS STITCH**

● **CROSS STITCH – ALTERNATE**

● **CROSS STITCH – DIAGONAL**

CROSS STITCH ● Victorian panel in wool framed as a picture

This chapter contains descriptions, diagrams and stitched samples of thirty-four crossed stitches, and six other embroidery stitches which can be used in conjunction with them. A crossed stitch is one that is formed by two or more stitches crossing each other. The angle of crossing can vary from the right angle of simple cross stitch to the oblique angle of herringbone stitch. The stitches range from easy-to-work cross stitch through to the complicated, interlaced Maltese cross, which requires more expertise. They are arranged alphabetically in families. A cross-referenced section at the end of the chapter lists the stitches which are suitable for working on canvas, even-weave or plain-weave fabrics.

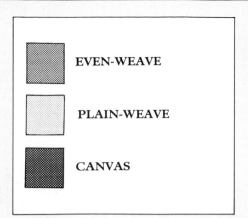

EVEN-WEAVE

PLAIN-WEAVE

CANVAS

BASKET STITCH

Basket stitch produces a braided effect and is useful for both fillings and edgings. It can be worked to give an open or closed finish and is used on plain-weave fabrics. It is a close stitch, worked with a forwards and backwards motion.

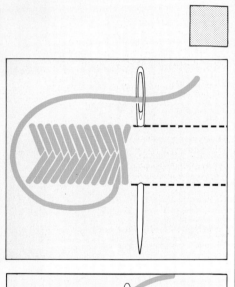

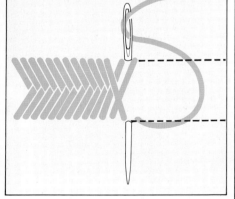

CROSS STITCH — also known as sampler stitch

Cross stitch is one of the best known of all embroidery stitches and is easy to work. It is extremely versatile, excellent for outlines, solid fillings, motifs and borders. The top diagonals should always be worked in the same direction, unless a deliberate light and shade effect is required, in which case their direction can be varied to catch the light.

Cross stitches can be worked individually, that is, a complete cross is worked before proceeding to the next one. This method produces neat, raised crosses. Cross stitch on canvas should always be worked in this way, on double canvas for the best results. It is essential that each cross stitch completely covers the canvas, so choice of thread is important.

Cross stitch can also be worked in rows, a method particularly suitable for plain- and even-weave fabrics. A line of diagonal stitches is worked in one direction and then covered on the second journey by a line worked in the other direction.

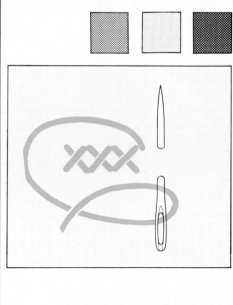

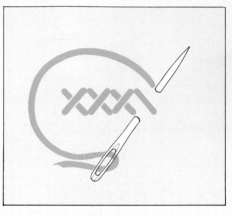

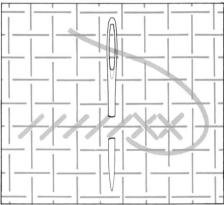

Cross stitch can also be worked in different combinations of half and threequarter stitches as shown below.

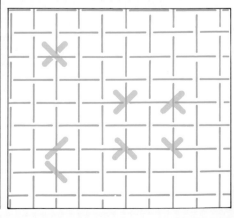

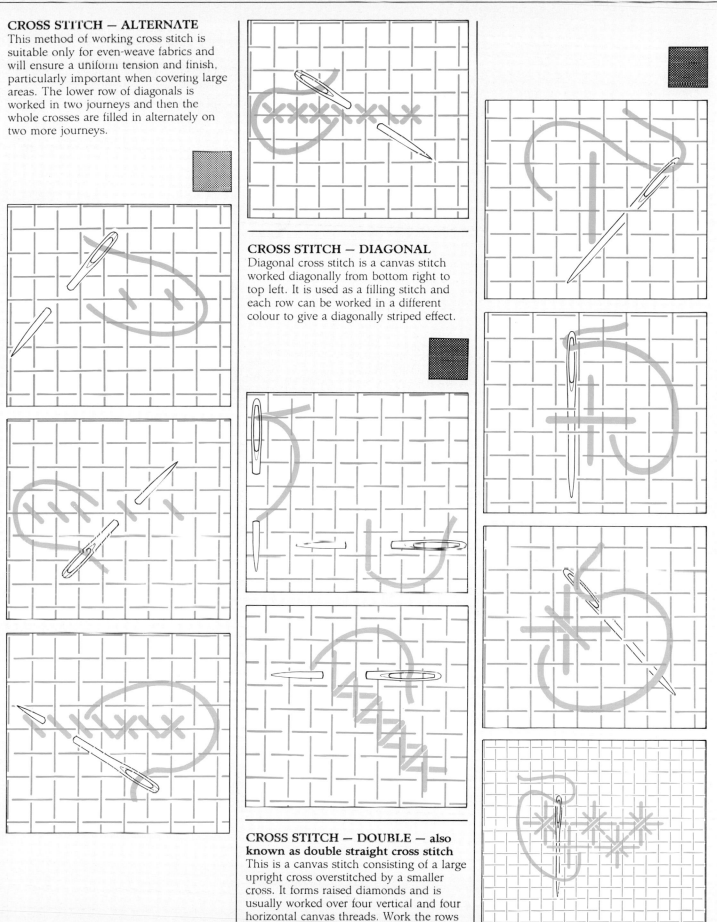

CROSS STITCH — ALTERNATE

This method of working cross stitch is suitable only for even-weave fabrics and will ensure a uniform tension and finish, particularly important when covering large areas. The lower row of diagonals is worked in two journeys and then the whole crosses are filled in alternately on two more journeys.

CROSS STITCH — DIAGONAL

Diagonal cross stitch is a canvas stitch worked diagonally from bottom right to top left. It is used as a filling stitch and each row can be worked in a different colour to give a diagonally striped effect.

CROSS STITCH — DOUBLE — also known as double straight cross stitch

This is a canvas stitch consisting of a large upright cross overstitched by a smaller cross. It forms raised diamonds and is usually worked over four vertical and four horizontal canvas threads. Work the rows from left to right and then right to left.

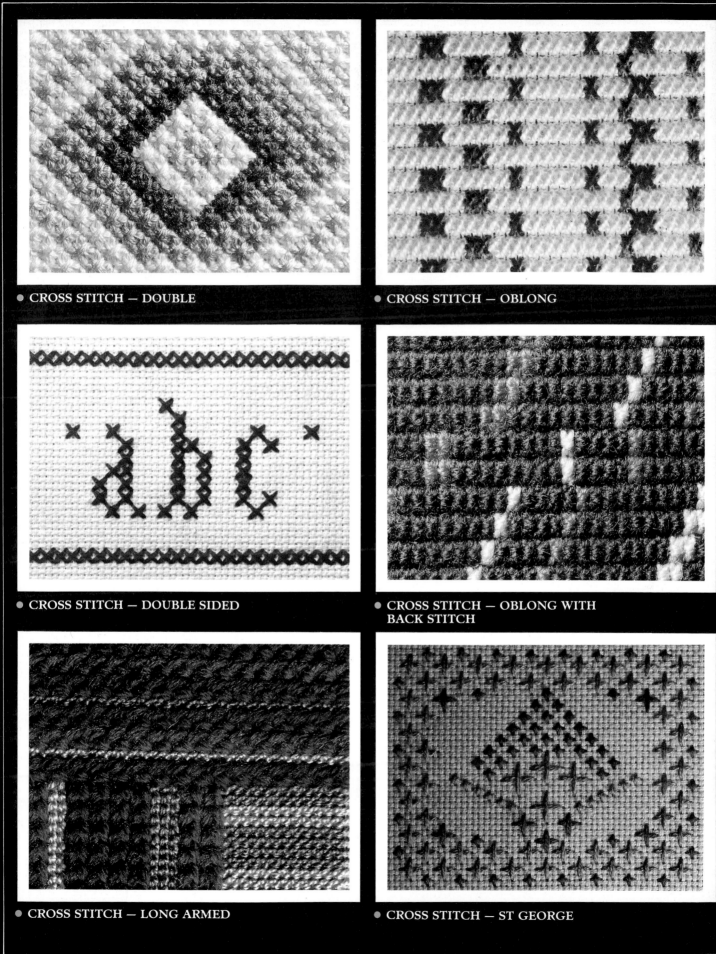

● CROSS STITCH — DOUBLE

● CROSS STITCH — OBLONG

● CROSS STITCH — DOUBLE SIDED

● CROSS STITCH — OBLONG WITH
  BACK STITCH

● CROSS STITCH — LONG ARMED

● CROSS STITCH — ST GEORGE

LONG ARMED STITCH • seventeenth-century Italian border in silk on linen

CROSS STITCH — DOUBLE SIDED

Double sided cross stitch makes an identical stitch on both sides of the fabric and is used on plain- and even-weave fabrics. It is an ideal form for fine, semi-transparent fabrics and for work which is reversible. Four journeys are needed to complete a single row, with half diagonals being worked at the end of the first journey and before the last (step 1 and step 5). The dotted lines show the stitches being made on the reverse side of the fabric. If it is necessary to re-cross a fully-made stitch to get to a point of continuation, this should be done as neatly as possible.

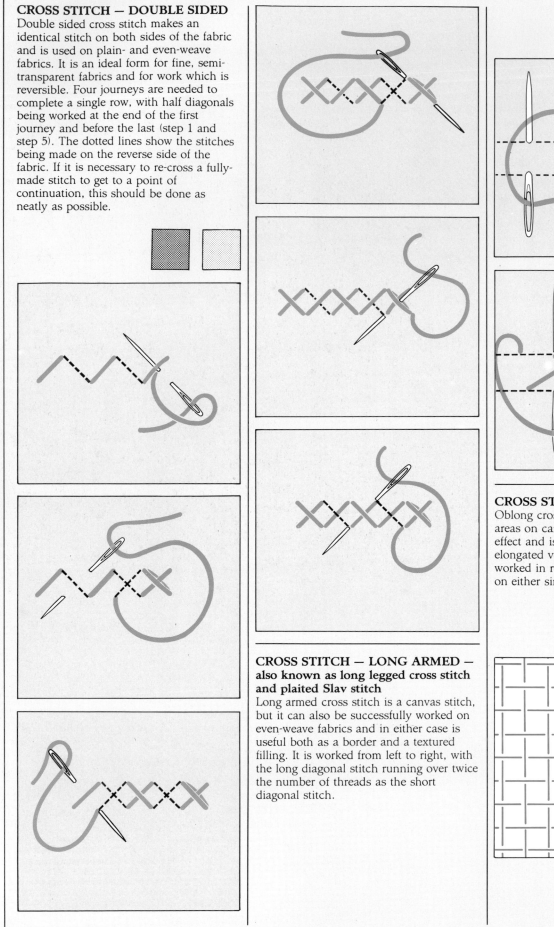

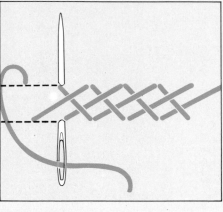

CROSS STITCH — OBLONG

Oblong cross stitch is used for filling large areas on canvas as it creates a neat, ridged effect and is quick to work. It is an elongated version of the basic cross stitch worked in rows rather than individually, on either single or double canvas.

CROSS STITCH — LONG ARMED — also known as long legged cross stitch and plaited Slav stitch

Long armed cross stitch is a canvas stitch, but it can also be successfully worked on even-weave fabrics and in either case is useful both as a border and a textured filling. It is worked from left to right, with the long diagonal stitch running over twice the number of threads as the short diagonal stitch.

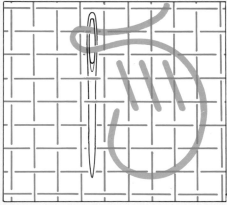

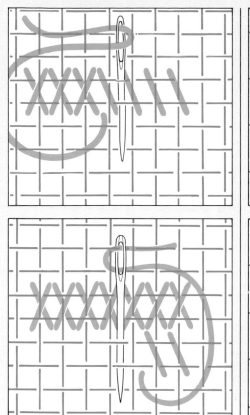

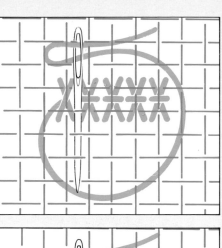

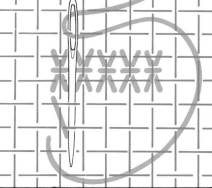

CROSS STITCH — ST GEORGE

This is an upright cross stitch used on plain- and even-weave fabrics. It is mainly used as a filling stitch, and the density can be varied by altering the spaces between each cross. It is worked as a row of horizontal stitches which are then crossed by vertical stitches of the same length.

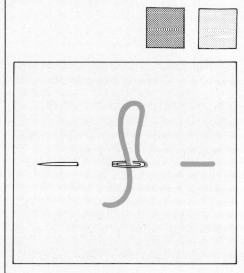

CROSS STITCH — OBLONG WITH BACK STITCH

This canvas stitch is very similar to oblong cross stitch, but gives a more crunchy texture over a large area. It is slower to work, as each cross is formed individually, with a back stitch across the centre. The rows can be worked in either direction and single canvas should be used.

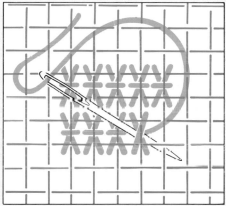

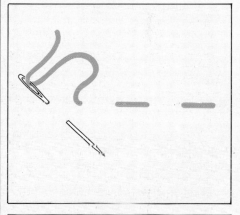

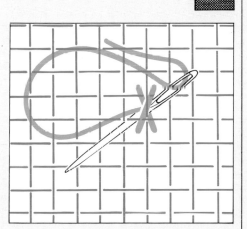

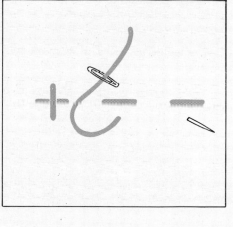

● ERMINE STITCH

● FLAT STITCH

● HERRINGBONE STITCH

● FERN STITCH

● FISHBONE STITCH

- **HERRINGBONE STITCH — CLOSED**   - **HERRINGBONE STITCH — DOUBLE**   - **HERRINGBONE STITCH — INTERLACED**

- **GREEK STITCH**

ERMINE STITCH

Ermine stitch is used on plain-weave fabrics for fillings and borders. Its name comes from the ermine tail effect it makes when worked in black thread on a white background. It consists of a long vertical stitch which is then covered by an elongated cross stitch about one-third shorter. The cross should be placed above the base of the vertical stitch.

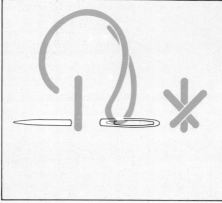

FERN STITCH

Fern stitch is a canvas stitch which forms plaited, vertical ridges and should be used on double canvas. Each row of top-heavy crosses must be worked from the top to the bottom of the canvas.

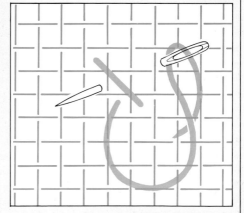

FISHBONE STITCH

Fishbone stitch makes an attractive chevron pattern and is worked on double canvas. Each stitch consists of a long diagonal held down at one end by a short crossing stitch.

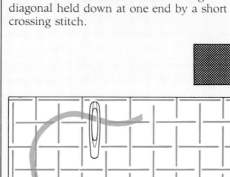

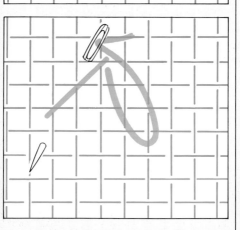

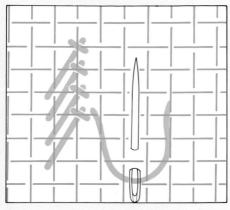

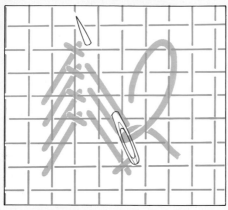

FLAT STITCH

Flat stitch is worked with a fairly thick thread on plain-weave fabrics. It is used for filling small shapes solidly or can be worked in parallel rows to give a heavy outline to a shape. It is always worked from the inner margin to the outer margin.

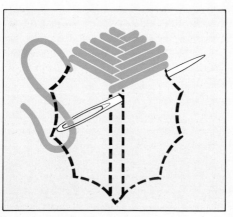

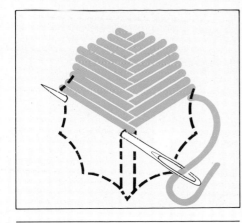

GREEK STITCH

Greek stitch is a canvas stitch which should be worked in a fairly coarse thread on either single or double canvas. It is similar to herringbone stitch, although the crosses are not spaced symmetrically, and it gives the effect of a plaited texture when applied over large areas.

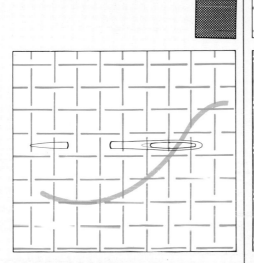

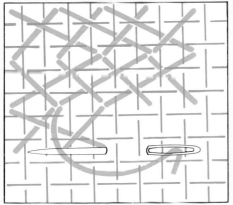

HERRINGBONE STITCH — also known as Russian stitch, Russian cross stitch and Mossoul stitch

Herringbone stitch is very simple and can be used on plain- and even-weave fabrics and canvas. It can be worked in single rows or as a filling and it forms the foundation row for a number of more complicated stitches.

HERRINGBONE STITCH — CLOSED — also known as shadow stitch and double back stitch

Closed herringbone stitch can be used in two distinct ways. It can be worked on plain- and even-weave fabrics as a border stitch to give a plaited effect. It is also used for shadow work on semi-transparent fabrics, with the rows of straight stitches appearing on the front of the work and the herringbone showing through the fabric in shadow form. It is worked in the same way as herringbone stitch, but the diagonals touch at the top and bottom.

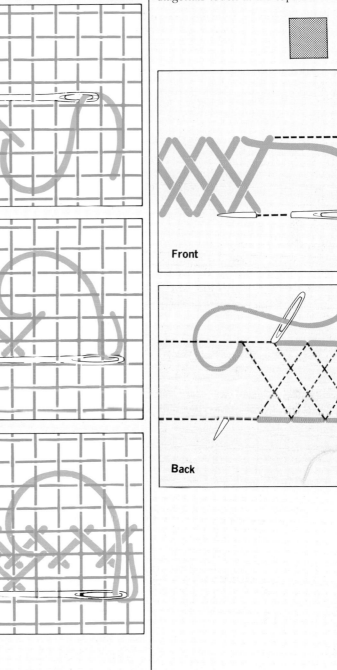

Front

Back

21

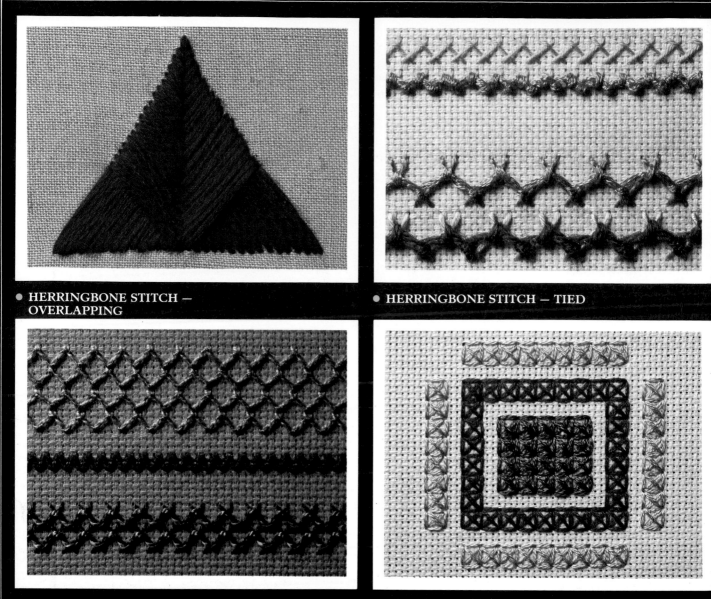

- **HERRINGBONE STITCH —
  OVERLAPPING**

- **HERRINGBONE STITCH — TIED**

- **HERRINGBONE STITCH —
  THREADED**

- **ITALIAN STITCH**

- **LEAF STITCH**

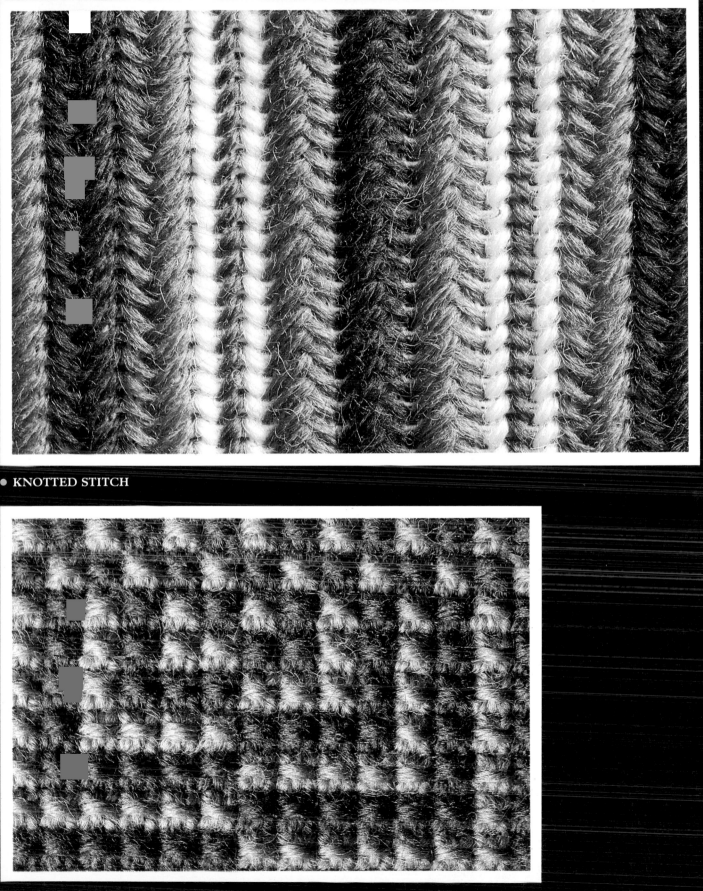

KNOTTED STITCH

LEVIATHAN STITCH

HERRINGBONE STITCH — DOUBLE

Double herringbone stitch can be worked on plain- and even-weave fabrics and canvas. It consists of a foundation row of basic herringbone with a second row, often a contrasting colour, worked over it.

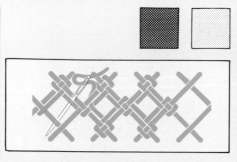

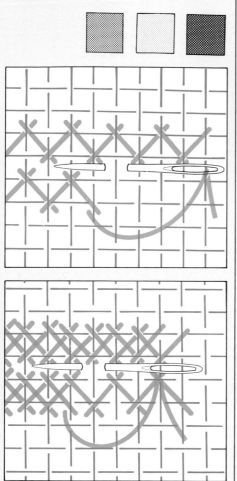

HERRINGBONE STITCH — INTERLACED

Interlaced herringbone stitch can be used as a rich border on plain- and even-weave fabrics, or as an insertion stitch to make a decorative seam joining two pieces of fabric together. The interlacing thread can contrast with the herringbone foundation and the stitch looks very rich when interlaced with metallic thread. The herringbone formation of the base is slightly different from the normal double herringbone stitch as the stitches on the second row are worked over and under those of the first row. The trick in working this stitch correctly is to study its formation carefully from the diagram and make sure the foundation herringbone is correct before proceeding to the interlacing. Work the foundation rows fairly loosely, as the interlacing will draw the stitches together. Thread the interlacing by working along one side and the middle of the row, and then work the second side and the middle.

HERRINGBONE STITCH — OVERLAPPING — also known as raised fishbone stitch

Overlapping herringbone stitch is used only on plain-weave fabrics and is a filling for shapes such as leaves and petals, triangles and lozenges, to give a padded and raised effect. It is worked over a straight central stitch at the top of the shape and built up with overlapping diagonal stitches worked from side to side and crossing in the centre. These stitches should be evenly placed and as close together as possible, to give a smooth surface to the raised area.

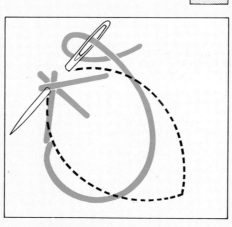

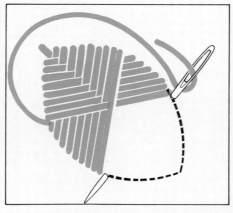

HERRINGBONE STITCH — THREADED

Threaded herringbone stitch can be used on plain- and even-weave fabrics as a simple two-colour border, or a rich background filling which can be laced with metallic thread. A row of basic herringbone stitch is worked first, then a second thread is laced upwards and downwards through the foundation stitches. When worked as a background, the foundation rows should touch at the tips of the crosses. The colour of the lacing thread can be varied to give a gradual colour change over the area.

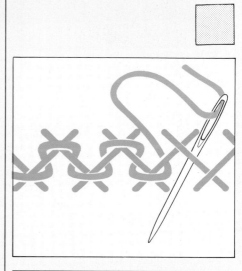

HERRINGBONE STITCH — TIED

Tied herringbone stitch is very similar to threaded herringbone. A row of basic herringbone is worked first and then the crosses are tied together using a contrasting thread and a simple knot.

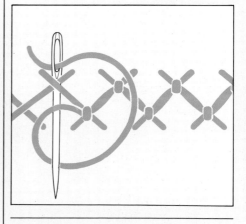

ITALIAN STITCH — also known as arrowhead cross stitch

Italian stitch, used primarily on canvas, consists of a cross surrounded by four straight stitches arranged in a square. When worked on loosely woven even-weave fabric, the stitches can be pulled together tightly for an openwork effect.

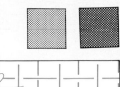

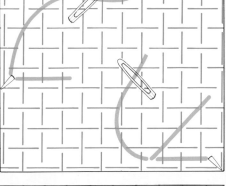

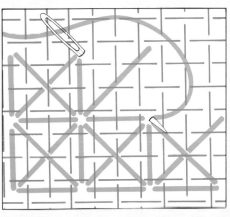

KNOTTED STITCH

Knotted stitch is used on double canvas for backgrounds and large areas. It consists of a long slanting stitch tied down by a short diagonal crossing stitch. The rows of stitching overlap to give a closely packed, ridged appearance.

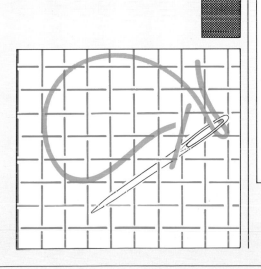

LEAF STITCH

Leaf stitch is a light, open stitch suitable for filling regular shapes and, unlike most other stitches, is always worked upwards. It is only used on plain-weave fabrics. It can also be used as a border and if the lengths of the stitches are varied the border is given an undulating line. An outline stitch, such as back stitch, is often worked round the edge of leaf stitch to define the shape distinctly.

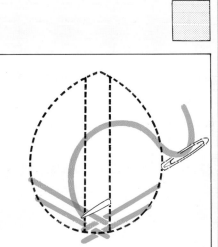

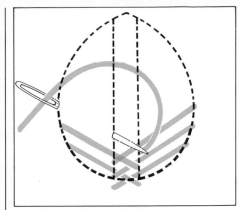

LEVIATHAN STITCH — also known as Smyrna cross stitch

Leviathan stitch is a canvas stitch consisting of an upright cross stitch over a basic cross stitch. It is usually worked over four horizontal and four vertical canvas threads and each stitch forms a neat, raised square unit. These units can be worked in alternate colours to give a chequerboard effect. Leviathan stitch is suitable for even-weave fabrics providing a fine thread is used.

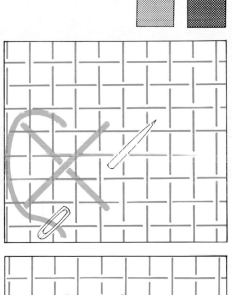

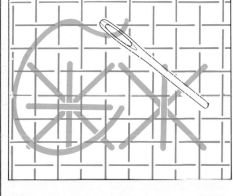

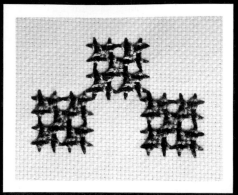

● MALTESE CROSS

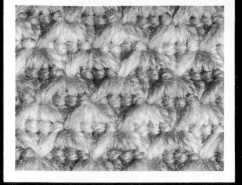

● ROCOCO STITCH

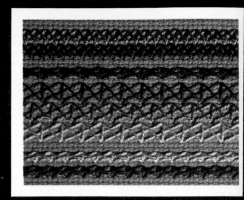

● MONTENEGRIN STITCH

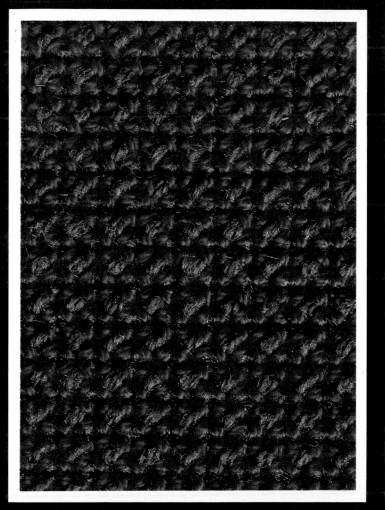

● RICE STITCH

● LEVIATHAN STITCH — DOUBLE

MONTENEGRIN STITCH ● English sampler of 1656 in coloured silks

LEVIATHAN STITCH — DOUBLE

Double Leviathan stitch looks similar to the ordinary version but has a much heavier, crunchy appearance. It is slightly more complicated, and the sequence of stitches shown in the diagram must be carefully followed.

MALTESE CROSS — also known as Maltese Cross interlacing stitch

Maltese cross is an intricate laced stitch used on plain- and even-weave fabrics. It can be worked as single motifs or as joined stitches to make a rich, heavy border. It is started by a framework of crossed stitches which must pass over and under each other in the sequence shown on the diagram. The interlacing will tighten them up, so work quite loosely at first to avoid puckering the fabric. This framework is then laced in a similar way to interlaced herringbone stitch, using either the same thread or one of a different colour or texture. The motifs can be joined at the corners or placed edge to edge.

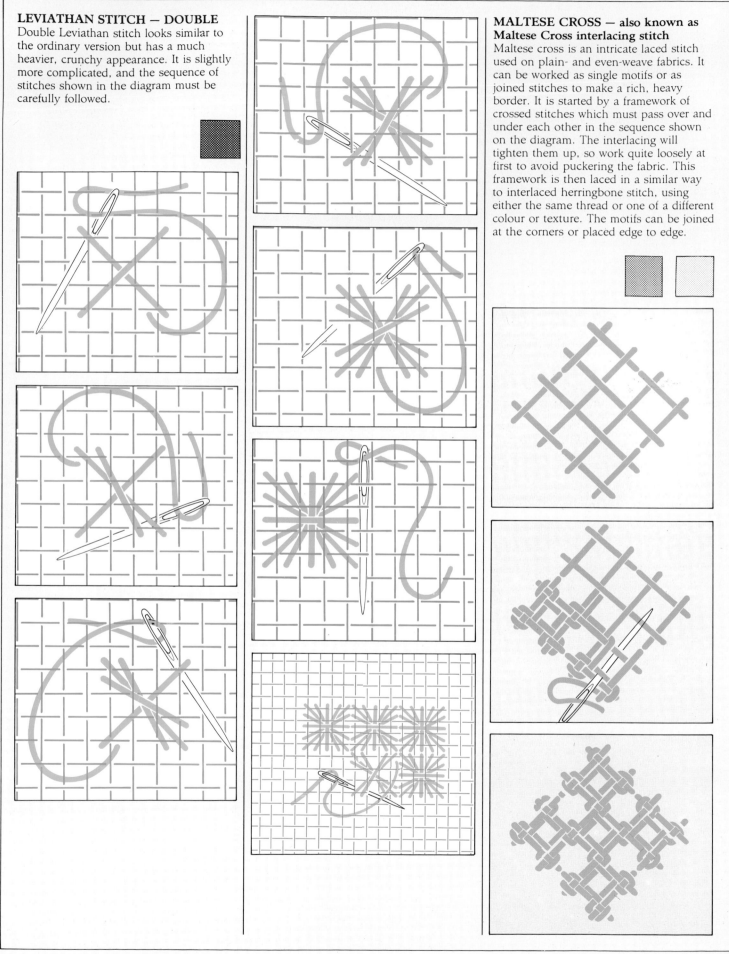

MONTENEGRIN STITCH

Montenegrin stitch is used on canvas and even-weave fabrics. The finished appearance is similar to long armed cross stitch with the addition of vertical bars. When this stitch is worked on canvas, a fairly coarse thread is necessary to cover the canvas completely.

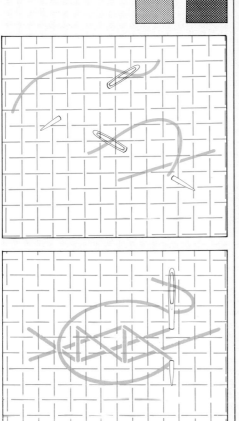

RICE STITCH — also known as William and Mary stitch and crossed corners cross stitch

Rice stitch is a canvas stitch with a dense texture and, as it covers the canvas well, can be used for large areas. It can be worked in two colours or two thicknesses of thread by forming the large crosses first and then stitching the corner diagonals with a second thread. If using two thicknesses of thread, use the thickest thread for the large crosses and the thinner one for the corners. Interesting shaded effects can be achieved by working an area of large crosses in one colour, and varying the colours of thread used for the corner stitches.

ROCOCO STITCH

Rococo stitch makes a dramatic background in canvaswork and should be worked on a wide mesh canvas with a fairly thick thread. It consists of four vertical stitches worked into the same space, tied down individually over one thread each with short crossing stitches. The vertical stitches curve when anchored into place on the canvas and make globe-shaped units.

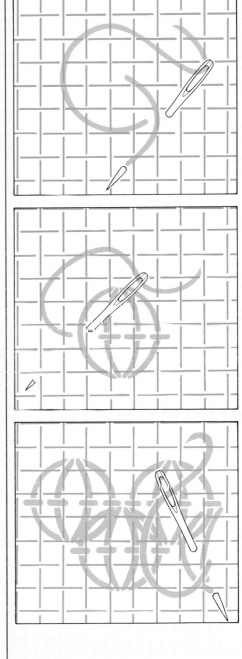

ROCOCO STITCH ● seventeenth-century English panel for a pincushion

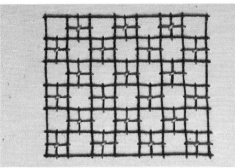

- **TOROCKO STITCH**

- **UNDERLINED STITCH**

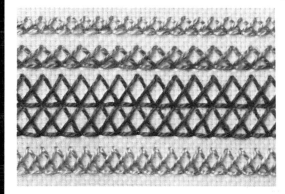

- **VELVET STITCH**

- **BACK STITCH**

TOROCKO STITCH

Torocko stitch is a quickly worked filling stitch used only on plain-weave fabrics. A foundation grid of evenly spaced long stitches is worked first, across the whole shape, and then covered with diagonal rows of upright crosses, with a short diagonal stitch worked from bottom left to top right to finish. The crosses can be worked in a different colour from that used to form the grid, with a third colour being used for the anchoring diagonal stitches.

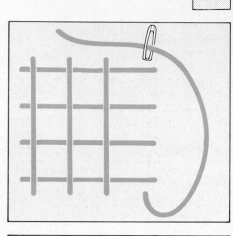

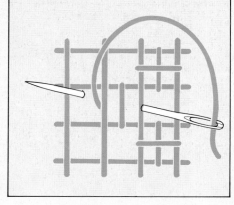

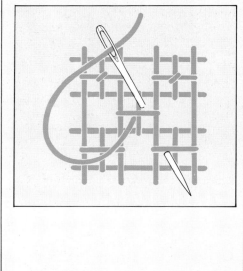

UNDERLINED STITCH

Underlined stitch is worked on canvas or even-weave fabrics. Each cross stitch is underlined by a horizontal straight stitch before the next cross is worked.

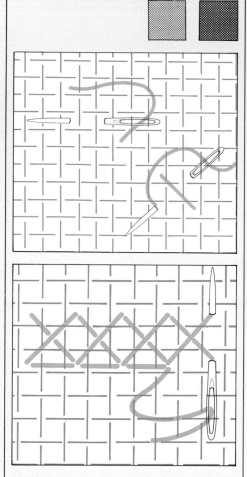

VELVET STITCH — also known as plush stitch

Velvet stitch resembles the pile of a carpet and is usually worked on double canvas. Use a thick wool or several strands of a fine wool through the needle at the same time. The loops are cut and trimmed to length after all the stitching has been completed. If the stitches are worked very closely together on the canvas in thick wool, the resulting pile will be dense enough to be sculptured into different levels with a sharp pair of scissors.

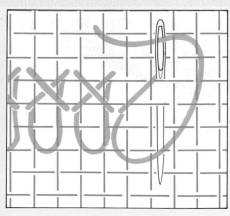

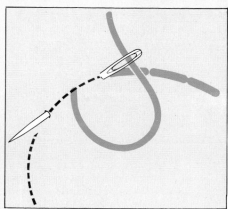

Other useful stitches

BACK STITCH — also known as point de sable stitch.

Back stitch is a slightly raised line stitch, worked from right to left on plain- and even-weave fabrics. It should be kept small and even and looks rather like machine stitching. It is also used as a foundation for other stitches, such as Pekinese stitch.

FRENCH KNOT — also known as dot stitch and knotted stitch

French knots are a little tricky at first and are best worked on a frame, to leave both hands free for twisting the thread round the needle. They are used mainly on plain weave fabrics for powdering and sprinkling effects, or worked solidly where texture is required. French knots can also accentuate details and add highlights to solid areas of stitching on canvas.

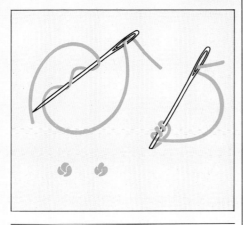

HOLBEIN STITCH — also known as double running stitch, stroke stitch and Romanian stitch

Holbein stitch is worked very simply and always on even-weave fabrics. A row of running stitch is worked first and on the return journey the spaces are filled in by a second row of the same stitch. This stitch is used in Assisi embroidery to outline the areas of cross stitch. It is similar to back stitch, but the finish is flat not raised.

LONG AND SHORT STITCH — also known as plumage stitch and shading stitch

Long and short stitch is a variation of satin stitch that gives a gradually shaded effect. It is also used to fill an area which is too large or irregular to be covered neatly by satin stitch and can be worked on plain- and even-weave fabrics and on canvas. The first row is made up of alternately long and short stitches which closely follow the outline of the shape to be filled. The subsequent rows are worked in satin stitches of equal length.

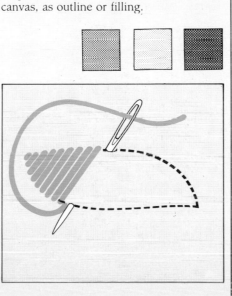

SATIN STITCH

Satin stitch appears easy, but some practice is required to work it neatly. The secret lies in making the stitches lie evenly and close together. It can be worked in varying lengths, but very long stitches may become loose and untidy. The stitches can be vertical or diagonal, with a change of direction giving the effect of light and shade. Satin stitch can be used on plain- and even-weave fabrics and on canvas, as outline or filling.

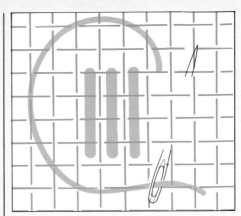

TENT STITCH — also known as petit point

Tent stitch is a canvas stitch used for fine work. It forms a small diagonal stitch which should always lie in the same direction. Tent stitch creates a flat, fairly smooth surface and combines well with heavier canvas stitches, accentuating their raised appearance.

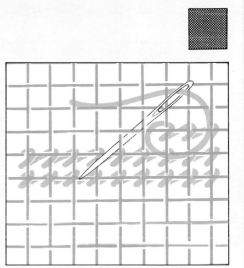

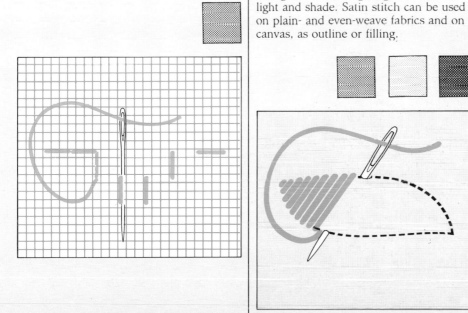

CUSHION COVERS

A cross stitch panel for a cushion cover is a simple project for inexperienced stitchers, but a large enough task to provide good practice in following a design and creating neat, regular stitching. The three designs shown here demonstrate very different approaches to the basic square format. A chequerboard design with bold geometric motifs covers the whole panel; a landscape picture in cross stitch is framed by a striped border of satin stitch; an abstract design contrasts vivid stripes with a border of plain colour, setting the smooth texture of stranded cotton against heavier stitching in tapestry wool. Basic sewing skills are needed for making up the cushions and directions are included for two methods of completion.

Other projects in the following pages may suggest ideas for cushions. The pincushions and the chair seat

are the designs most simply adapted to the scale of a cushion pad. Alternatively, you can chart your own design to include your favourite motifs and patterns; if you particularly enjoy border patterns, for example, you could create a complex squared border and leave the centre of the panel plain, reversing the emphasis of the bordered designs shown here.

Landscape picture cushion

In this design the landscape is framed by the heavy border, as if seen through a window. The picture is 6 in (15 cm) square, with a 3 in (7.5 cm) border on either side, making the design 12 in (30 cm) square overall, to fit a standard size of cushion pad. You can apply the design to a larger cushion by repeating the satin stitch stripes to extend the border.

MATERIALS
Cushion pad 12 in (30 cm) square
Double-weave canvas, 10 gauge
Stranded cottons 1 skein of each colour
  light brown
  dark brown
  mid-green
  olive green
  light blue
  shaded blue
  4 tones of grey from
  silver grey to charcoal
Tapestry wools 5 skeins of brown
  4 skeins of green
  2 skeins of dusty
  pink
Crewel and tapestry needles
Embroidery frame or stretcher
Heavy cotton or light wool backing fabric
Sewing needle and thread

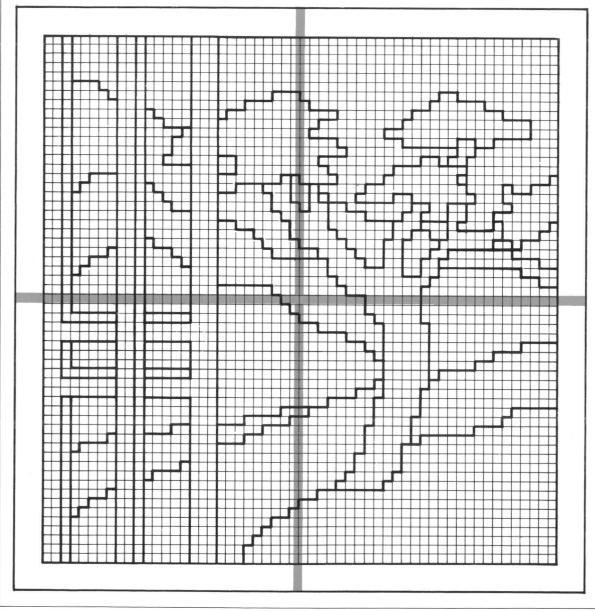

This chart shows the central section of the landscape picture design, which is worked entirely in cross stitch. One square of the chart represents one stitch. The embroidery is worked from the centre outwards. The vertical and horizontal axes are marked to locate the central point.

METHOD

Stretch the canvas on the frame. The area of stitching is 12 in (30 cm) square and you should allow a margin of 3 in (7.5 cm) of canvas all around. Tack in the central lines on the canvas and start stitching the picture, from the centre outwards, using cross stitch and six strands of cotton. When the picture is complete, work the striped border in satin stitch with the tapestry wools.

FINISHING

Block the embroidery, if necessary. Trim the canvas to a margin of 1¼ in (3 cm) on each side of the design. Cut a piece of backing fabric the same size as the canvas. Put the canvas and backing fabric right sides together and pin the edges. Machine stitch seams on three sides, 1¼ in (3 cm) from the edges, and turn the stitching just around each corner on the fourth side. Clip diagonally across the corners of the seams, turn the cover to the right side and press the seams, paying special attention to the corners which should be pushed out to square off the shape cleanly. Insert the cushion pad and close up the open side of the cover with handstitching. To make a removable cover, sew press studs or Velcro inside the open edge.

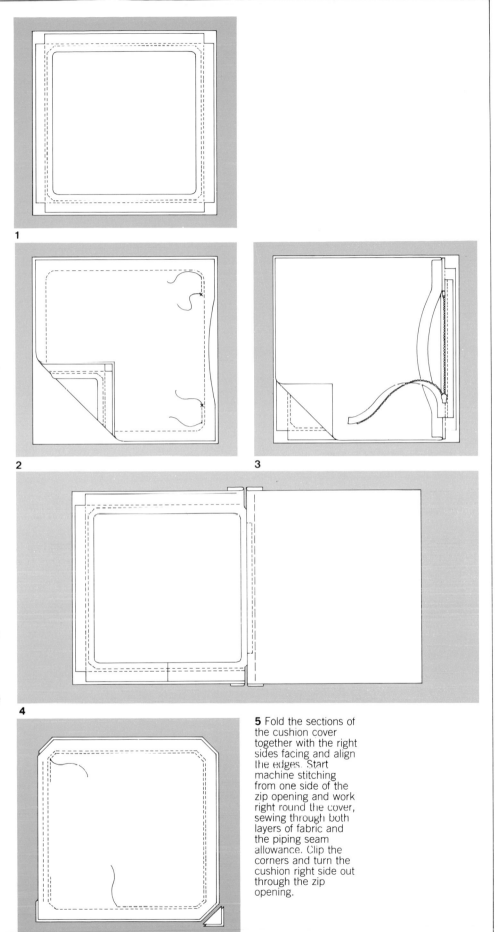

Making up a piped cushion cover
1 Arrange the piping around the right side of one section of the cover. Tack it down and nick the seam allowance at the corners. Stitch the piping in place.
2 On the wrong side of the same section, mark the opening for the zip. Put the two sections of the cover right sides together and machine stitch on either side of the zip opening, as far as the corner seams.
3 Open the zip and pin one side to the seam allowance of the zip opening. Machine stitch it in place.
4 Close the zip and tack across the width at either end. Open out the cover sections, right side up. Stitch the free end of the zip to the second seam allowance of the zip opening. Remove the tacking threads and open the zip.

5 Fold the sections of the cushion cover together with the right sides facing and align the edges. Start machine stitching from one side of the zip opening and work right round the cover, sewing through both layers of fabric and the piping seam allowance. Clip the corners and turn the cushion right side out through the zip opening.

Striped panel cushion

The basic construction of this design is really quite simple, but the effect is very striking. A pattern of regular stripes is interrupted by small blocks shifted out of alignment or imposed diagonally and horizontally on the vertical pattern. To create an alternative design, varying the colourways or widths of the stripes, paint stripes on paper and cut out small blocks, leaving a broad area of pattern. Arrange the blocks on the striped area, moving and turning the shapes until you arrive at a pleasing design. Trim the small pieces to shape as necessary and chart the full design on graph paper.

MATERIALS

Cushion pad 12 in (30 cm) square
Double-weave canvas, 10 gauge
Stranded cottons 1 skein of each colour
              silver grey
              charcoal grey
              royal blue
              black
Black tapestry wool
Crewel and tapestry needles
Embroidery frame or stretcher
Heavy cotton or light wool backing fabric

METHOD

Copy the design on graph paper, charting one square of the graph to one woven block of canvas. The striped section is 5 in (12.5 cm) square and the panel is made up to the size of the cushion pad by the wide border all around.

    Stretch the canvas on the embroidery frame and tack in the central lines. Work the striped panel from your chart, in cross stitch using six strands of cotton. When the central design is complete, work the border in tapestry wool. The border stitches are Leviathan stitch and oblong cross stitch with back stitch, alternating in double rows, up to the last eight rows, which are all oblong cross stitch with back stitch.

FINISHING

Finish the cover by the instructions given for the Landscape Picture Cushion above.

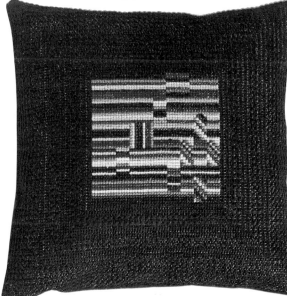

Chequerboard motif cushion

This cushion cover features 16 different geometric motifs, each set in a square of colour to form a chequerboard pattern. The motifs are linked visually by the use of a limited colour scheme. The design for the cushion cover differs from the previous two, in that the embroidered panel is mounted on a separately made fabric cover and finished with a braid trim, rather than forming one complete side of the cover.

    The design can be interpreted in different ways by a simple change of scale. If the embroidery is worked on 14 gauge canvas instead of the 7 gauge used in the

original, and stitched in finer wool, the complete design can be stitched four times in the same area, giving 64 motifs in all. Alternatively, it can be simplified: for example, by stitching alternate squares in a plain colour and using only half the number of motifs.

MATERIALS

Cushion pad 15 in (38 cm) square
Double-weave canvas, 7 gauge
Tapestry wools 5 skeins of each colour
                white
                bright pink
                yellow ochre
                light brown
                1 skein of black
                2 skeins of dull mauve
Tapestry needle
Embroidery frame or stretcher
Heavy cotton or light wool fabric for the cushion cover
Braid
Piping
12 in (30 cm) zip
Sewing needle and thread

METHOD

Work directly from the chart or copy the design onto graph paper. The finished area of stitching is just under 14 in (35 cm) square and you should allow a margin of 3 in (7.5 cm) of canvas all around. Stretch the canvas on the frame, tack in the central lines and work the design from the chart, using cross stitch throughout.

FINISHING

Take the canvas off the frame and block it. When it is thoroughly dry, trim the margin to ½ in (1.5 cm) all around. This margin must be covered by the braid you have chosen to edge the design, so trim it more closely if necessary.

Cut two pieces of fabric 17½ in (44 cm) square, which includes seam allowances of 1¼ in (3 cm). On the right side of the piece, centre the embroidery and pin it in place. Tack round the edge of the canvas, close to the stitching. Tack braid around the edge of the embroidery, covering the raw edges of the canvas and mitring the braid at each corner. Stitch the braid in place by hand or machine.

Make up the cushion cover as shown in the diagrams, inserting piping in the seams and a zip to close the opening. You can buy piping readymade, or make it up specially by covering piping cord with strips of the fabric used for the cushion cover. This method of finishing gives a more formal appearance and you can unzip the cover to remove the cushion pad, but if you prefer a simpler method of making up, omit the piping and follow the instructions given for the Landscape Picture Cushion.

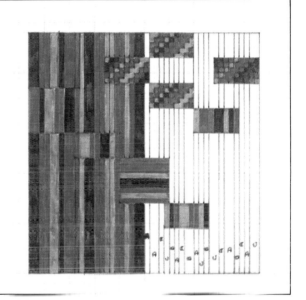

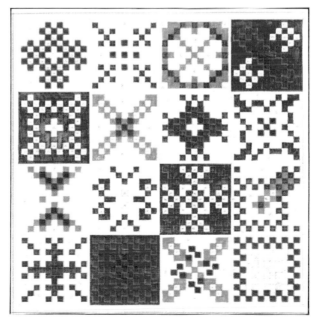

KEY TAGS

Small items such as these two key tags are quick to work and ideal for using up oddments of canvas and threads. The tags are worked on rigid plastic canvas, which can be held in the hand rather than on a frame while you are stitching and has the added advantage of not requiring stiffening. In these examples the front and back are worked separately and the design appears only on one side. Design problems are simplified in such a small area and a project on this scale is a useful vehicle for trying new motifs and fancy stitches.

Initial key tag

To make a personalized key tag, select your initial from the alphabet given here, look through the book for a different letter style, or chart one to your own design. Note that the letters in the alphabet have different widths. If your own initial is a wider letter than the J shown here — M or O, for example — you may need to broaden the shape of the whole tag to accommodate the design. You could, alternatively, develop a monogram using two or more initials, insert a tiny floral motif, or edge the design with a border.

MATERIALS

Plastic canvas, 10 gauge
Tapestry wool 1 skein of cream
              oddments of scarlet, bright
              pink and purple
Tapestry needle
Metal split ring

METHOD

Work the front and back of the tag following the chart. The initial is worked in rice stitch, otherwise tent stitch is used throughout. Do not press the finished embroidery as a warm iron will damage the plastic canvas.

FINISHING

Trim the canvas close to the stitching, as shown by the trim line on the chart. Place the two pieces wrong sides together and stitch the edges together with overcast stitch (see diagram). Thread the split ring through the top.

Nine-stitch key tag

The basic chequerboard pattern of this design is enlivened by the heavy texture of double Leviathan stitch. The monochrome colour scheme enhances the contrast between the raised centre and the flat area of tent stitch surrounding it. A strong contrast — white or a very pale colour against a clear, bright hue — could also prove effective if you want to accentuate the inner squares.

MATERIALS

Plastic canvas, 10 gauge
Tapestry wool 1 skein of light blue
              oddments of royal blue
              and turquoise
Tapestry needle
Metal split ring

METHOD

Work the front and back of the tag separately, using double Leviathan stitch to make the blocks and tent stitch for the border and the plain back. Do not press the finished work.

FINISHING

Make up and neaten the tag with overcast stitch, as described above.

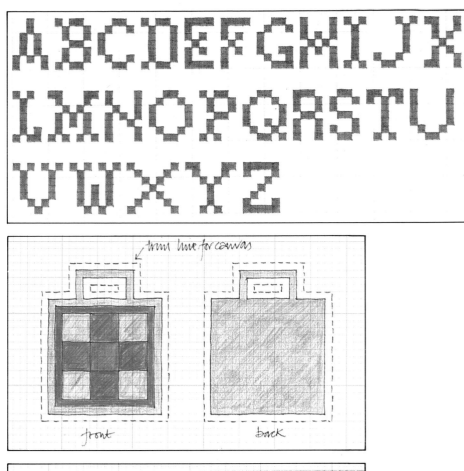

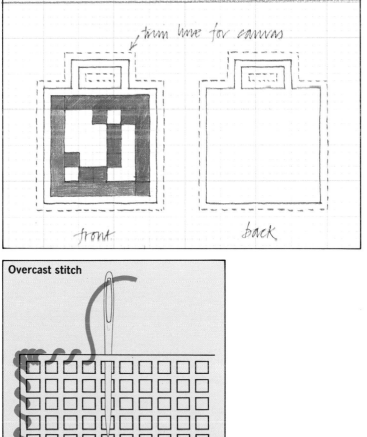

Overcast stitch

REPEAT PATTERN PURSE

This purse is made from a long rectangle of canvas, folded into three to form the two sides and the flap. Each section has the same geometric design, so all you need do is follow the chart and repeat the pattern three times. You require basic sewing skills to complete the project: the purse is given a neat finish with a lining, cord edging and a button fastening.

The choice of colours is a personal one and you can quickly trace off the design and try out different colour combinations on paper, using paint or felt-tip markers. By repeating the design blocks side by side as well as vertically, you can adapt the idea to a larger purse or evening bag, following the same procedure for making up. To add a glittering touch, consider using metallic threads or beadwork to decorate some of the shapes.

MATERIALS

Double-weave canvas, 10 gauge
Tapestry wools 1 skein of each colour
           dark blue
           royal blue
           pale blue
           pink
           lilac
Tapestry needle
Lining fabric
Thin cord in dark blue
Button
Sewing needle and thread.

METHOD

The basic design is a rectangle 3 x 3½ in (7.5 x 9 cm), repeated three times to form a piece 9 x 3½ in (23 x 9 cm). Follow the chart, working cross stitch throughout. One square of the design corresponds to one woven square in the canvas.

FINISHING

Lay the finished piece flat and trim the canvas to leave a ½ in (1.5 cm) margin on each side. Turn in the edges over the back of the embroidery and mitre the corners.

Cut a piece of lining fabric slightly larger than the canvaswork and turn in the raw edges. Slipstitch the lining to the back of the embroidery.

Stitch cord all around the edge of the rectangle. At the centre of one of the short sides of the rectangle, make a loop with e cord. This end of the fabric will form the purse flap and the cord loop will serve as a buttonhole. To finish the cord neatly, tuck the ends underneath the lining.

Fold the embroidery into three and stitch together two sections of the canvas on either side. Conceal the stitches as well as you can by working along the inner edge of the cord. Fold the flap down on the front of the purse and sew on a button to align with the loop of cord.

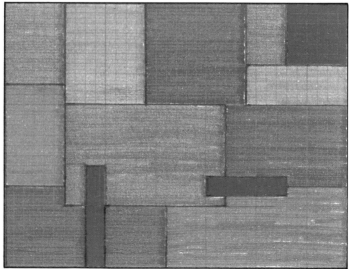

TABLECLOTH AND NAPKINS

The pattern for this tablecloth, inspired by a Thirties style of design, consists of a motif repeated in blocks of four and embroidered alternately in green and orange. The heavily embroidered corner sections are balanced by a narrow border strip at the centre of each side of the cloth, constructed from four motifs joined together. The napkins each have a single motif placed in one corner.

The cloth and napkins are made from white Hardanger, an even-weave fabric. The tablecloth is square, but you can easily work the design on a rectangular cloth by extending the central borders slightly to link the corner designs. Alternatively, you can work on a readymade tablecloth, if the threads of the fabric are regular and the weave clearly visible.

MATERIALS

Hardanger even-weave fabric, 22 gauge, in white
Stranded cottons 10 skeins of each colour
green
orange
Crewel needle
Sewing needle and white thread

METHOD

The embroidery is designed for a cloth 1 yd (90 cm) square and napkins 13 in (33 cm) square. Whether you work to these dimensions or choose your own, allow 4 in (10 cm) as a hem allowance on each side of the tablecloth and 1½ in (4 cm) on each side of the napkins.

Before beginning the embroidery, tack a row of stitching around the cloth 8 in (20 cm) from the edges. Use this as a guideline for placing the corner patterns and borders. The single motifs for the napkins are placed approximately 4 in (10 cm) from the edges. Follow the chart to work the embroidery in cross stitch, using three strands of cotton. The chart is calculated on the basis of one square of the graph to four woven blocks in the fabric.

FINISHING

When the embroidery is complete, press the fabric lightly. Turn a hem of 4 in (10 cm) of fabric onto the wrong side of the tablecloth, mitring the corners neatly as you stitch the hem in place. Make a hem with 1½ in (4 cm) of fabric on each napkin.

Mitring corners on fabric *(right)*
1 Fold over a narrow hem along the two edges of the fabric and press. Trim off the corner to avoid bulk, then turn over the corner.
2 Fold in the two sides to make a neat corner. Hem along the two turned in edges and along the diagonal join if you have a wide hem.

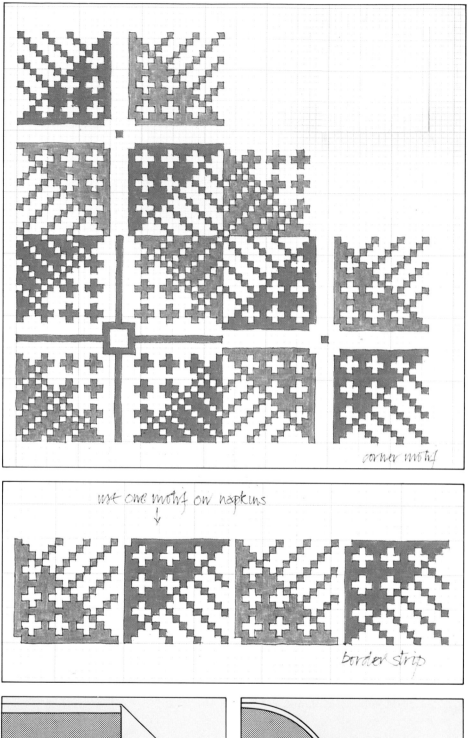

corner motif

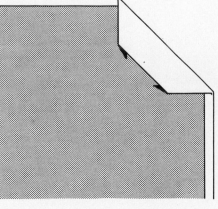

use one motif on napkins

border strip

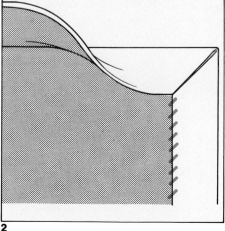

1

2

LAMPSHADE BORDER

A plain-coloured lampshade is enlivened by an embroidered border, completed on plastic canvas and attached to the lower edge of the shade. It is made from four separate pieces joined together with braided cross stitch. As the plastic canvas is rigid you can cut the pieces to shape and there is no need to work on a frame. The border is designed for a lampshade which is square at the lower edge but you can easily adapt the idea for a rounded shade, and change the colours to suit the scheme of your furnishings.

MATERIALS

Lampshade, 8 in (20 cm) square at the lower edge
Plastic canvas, 9 gauge
Stranded cottons 1 skein of each colour
           light green
           olive green
           light pink
           dark pink
           grey-blue
Tapestry needle
Felt
Sewing needle and invisible thread

METHOD

Cut the plastic canvas into four strips 8 in (20 cm) and 1½ in (4 cm) deep. On each strip, cut indentations in the lower edge at every alternate group of four threads, to make the geometric design as shown. Trim off the nubs of plastic to give the edging a smooth finish.

Follow the charted design, using six strands of cotton and cross stitch throughout. Each strip is bound at the top with braided cross stitch (see diagram) and finished at the lower edge with overcast stitch, again using six strands of cotton.

FINISHING

Cut strips of felt slightly smaller than the border sections and glue them to the back of the plastic canvas, using a fabric adhesive. Leave to dry thoroughly.

Join the four strips at the short ends with braided cross stitch. When the border is complete, attach it to the lower edge of the lampshade with small running stitches of invisible thread.

Braided cross stitch

BORDER PATTERN BELT

The design for this belt consists of a simple repeat pattern of interlocking L-shapes within a basic square. You can thus make the belt of a suitable length for your waist size by reworking the pattern as many times as is necessary. The blocks are bordered with heavy stripes which are also worked at each end of the belt to finish off the pattern. The colours used in the original design are close-toned, but the contrast created by setting a warm, bright rust against the clean blues and greens gives a rich, glowing effect. If you alter the colours, try to create a similar balance; you might choose a range of pastel hues to match a summer dress or dark, plummy tones for a winter outfit. Bright primary and secondary colours, as used in some styles of peasant embroidery, would make a striking accessory for a dress in black, white or a strong, plain colour.

A simple strip pattern of this kind can be adapted to other accessories, such as a choker or wristband, or you could alternatively apply it to furnishings — as a pull-cord or upholstery trimming, for example.

MATERIALS

Single-weave canvas, 18 gauge
Stranded cotton 1 skein of each colour
              black
              emerald green
              olive green
              royal blue
              rust
Crewel needle
Embroidery frame or stretcher
Belt buckle
Petersham ribbon or purchased belt stiffening
Sewing needle and thread

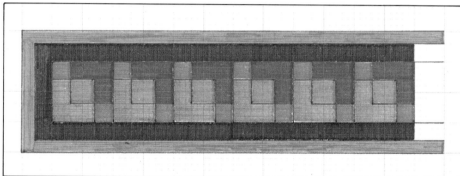

METHOD

The belt is just under 1¼ in (3 cm) wide but to avoid pulling the canvas out of shape as you work, stretch a broader section on a frame and trim it when the cross stitching is finished. Work cross stitch throughout with the needle threaded with three strands of cotton. Follow the chart, working section by section until you have the required length.

FINISHING

Remove the canvas from the frame and trim it to within ½ in (1.5 cm) all around the stitched area. Turn in the raw edges and mitre the corners (see diagram).

To attach the buckle, fold the end of the belt over the buckle bar and stitch the edges of the fold. Cut the ribbon or belt stiffening to the correct length and pin it to the wrong side of the belt. Secure it in place with small stitches along each edge.

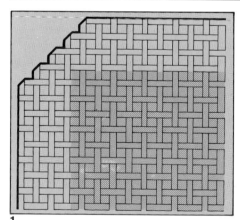

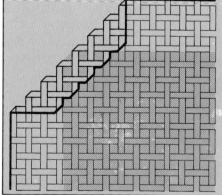

Mitring corners on canvas
1 Trim the corner of the surplus canvas to avoid excess bulk.
2 Turn over the cut canvas to the corner of the embroidery.
3 Fold in the side edges and stitch down the diagonal join, making sure the corner is square.

BORDERS FOR BEDLINEN

Embroidered gingham makes a decorative edging for a sheet and pillowcase. The cross stitch designs are repeated on strips of gingham — three centred pattern blocks for the sheet and two corner motifs for the pillow — which are sewn in place when the embroidery is complete. You can vary the design by repeating the motifs along the whole strip, or concentrating the embroidery at the corners of the sheet rather than at the centre. The design can be used for a duvet cover or scaled down for a cot sheet and there are several attractive colours of gingham to choose from, to match different coloured bedlinen. The embroidery colours consist of two tones closely related to the gingham and two which contrast, a balanced scheme which can be applied to other colour ranges.

MATERIALS

Brown cotton sheet and pillowcase
Brown and white gingham
Stranded cottons 1 skein of each colour
           dark brown
           rust
           olive green
           deep yellow
Crewel needle
Sewing thread

METHOD

Measure the sheet and pillowcase and cut strips of gingham to fit across the width, to make a border 8½ in (21 cm) deep on the sheet and 4½ in (11 cm) deep on the pillowcase. These measurements can be adapted to your requirements, but make sure you can fit the cross stitch design comfortably within the strip. To avoid wasting fabric, you can cut shorter strips and machine stitch them together to the required length, making a neat seam with the gingham checks precisely matched.

Turn in and tack a hem of ½ in (1.5 cm) on either side of each strip. Find the centre of the sheet border and stitch the first pattern block, using cross stitch and three strands of cotton. In the charted design, one square of the grid is equivalent to one square of the gingham. Work the pattern block twice more, evenly spaced on either side of the central block. Work the smaller motifs at each end of the gingham strip cut to fit the pillowcase.

FINISHING

When the embroidery is complete, lightly press the strips of gingham with a warm iron. Stitch them by hand or machine to the sheet and pillowcase, leaving a margin of plain fabric at the edge.

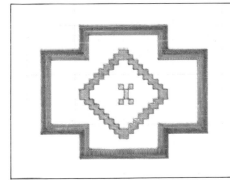

CANVASWORK CHAIR SEAT

Canvaswork in tapestry wool makes a suitable covering for chair seats as it is extremely hard-wearing and easy to mount on dining-chair seats, or on soft easy chairs. The chair shown here has a drop-in seat, which is the simplest type to attempt. In the following pages you will find different methods for seating a wood-frame chair with the canvaswork panel; alternatively, you can stitch it to the upholstery of a chair cushion, sofa back or footstool.

Many embroidery designs are suitable for upholstery, but small, all-over geometric designs and stripes are the most effective. They can be fitted to the tapering seat of a dining chair and even a simple geometric pattern offers plenty of scope for choosing attractive colour combinations. Assuming that the chair is frequently in use, it is best to choose deep colours for the largest areas of stitching and highlight the design with paler tones.

To work out the design area for your chair seat, remove the original covering and measure the seat carefully. Allow an extra ½ in (1.5 cm) of embroidery all round, where the seat fits into the wood frame, to ensure that no canvas shows around the stitching. The materials below will serve as a guide, but you should work a small test piece on a spare section of canvas to calculate how much thread will be required for your particular project. It is always preferable to overestimate thread quantities for a large piece of canvaswork, as dye lots vary considerably and you may find it difficult to match the wools if you run out.

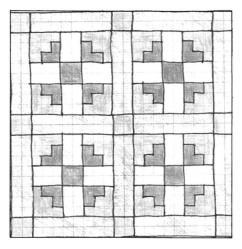

Covering a chair seat

1 Strip any old upholstery from the chair seat, leaving the wood base and foam padding. Cover the foam with lining fabric, securing the lining with tacks on the underside of the seat. Pull the fabric over the corners and tack it.

2 Neaten each corner by folding in the fabric at either side. Crease it firmly with your fingers.

3 Push aside the folds and trim off the triangle of fabric underneath.

4 Put the folded sections back in place and hammer in tacks. If the folds are not neatly creased, press them with a damp cloth before tacking. Neaten all four corners in the same way.

5 Spread out the canvaswork face downwards and place the chair seat on top, also right side down. Centre it on the canvas and fold the edges of the canvaswork over the back of the frame. Secure the edges with tacks, working outwards from the centre of each edge and stretching the canvas gently into shape. Neaten the corners with folds, in the same way as for the lining fabric.

6 To finish off the underside of the seat, tack hessian across the wood frame. Stretch it evenly across the back of the seat and turn under the raw edges and corners neatly.

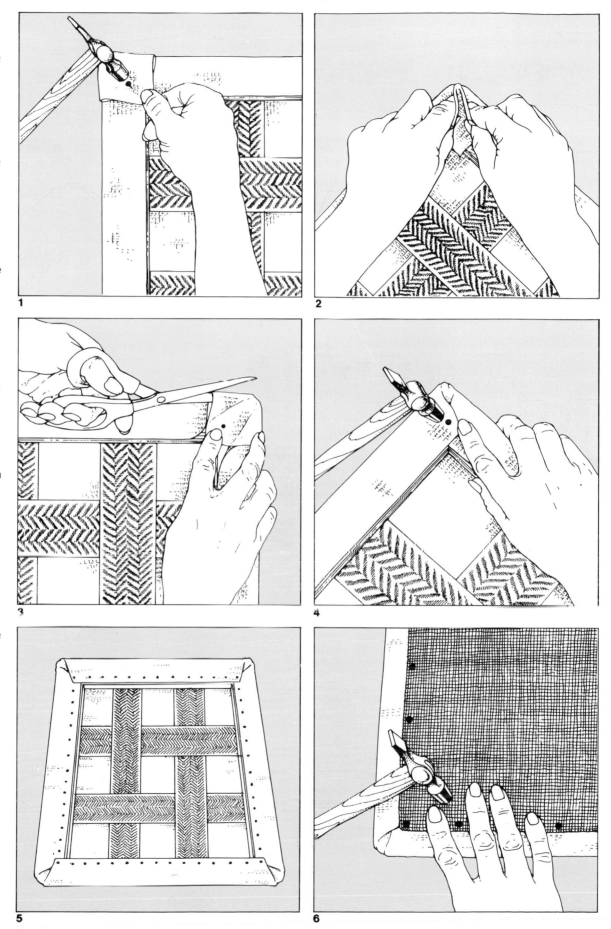

MATERIALS

Double-weave canvas, 10 gauge
Tapestry wools 6 skeins rust
                 7 skeins light blue
                 9 skeins mid-blue
                 9 skeins dark beige
Tapestry needle
Embroidery frame or stretcher
Hessian
Cotton lining fabric
Sewing needle and tacking thread
Hammer and tacks *or* staplegun

METHOD

The chair seat shown measures 18 in (45 cm) at the front and sides, tapering to 14 in (35 cm) at the back edge. The canvaswork is stitched in a repeat pattern of simple blocks, so you can calculate how many blocks you should work to fit your own chair seat.

Stretch the canvas on the embroidery frame. Tack the outline of the stitching area on canvas, allowing a margin of 8 in (20 cm) all around. Mark the centre point of the design with vertical and horizontal tacking threads.

Start stitching at the centre of the canvas, using the charted design as a guide. Work the areas of mid-blue and light blue in slanting satin stitch first, then fill in the beige and tan areas using Leviathan stitch.

FINISHING

When the embroidery is completed, remove it from the frame and block it. Allow it to dry thoroughly. Mount the canvaswork panel on the chair seat as shown in the diagrams.

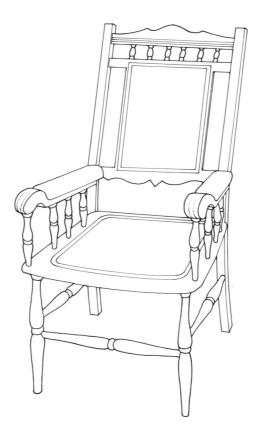

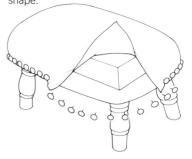

Different types of wood frame chairs are suitably upholstered with canvaswork. Some styles have a panel fitted on seat and back (*left*). The canvaswork is stretched directly onto the frame and tacked in place, with decorative braid concealing the raw edges. Canvaswork can be used to cover a small stool (*below*), secured at the base with pins. Pucker the edges of the canvas slightly to fit it snugly around the curved shape.

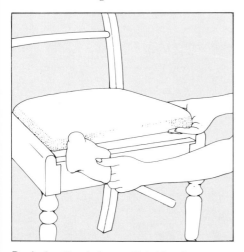

Replacing the chair seat The new covering on the chair seat may be difficult to fit at first. Wrap a hammer in clean cloth so you can tap the seat gently into place if necessary without damaging the canvaswork. Fit the back edge first and then ease in the sides and front.

Right Victorian embroiderers stitched panels of Berlin woolwork for chair seats and cushions favouring floral designs and pictorial motifs. As in this example, the flower patterns were particularly suited to seat panels with a curving or rounded shape.